TERRORISM
IN AMERICA

TRICIA ANDRYSZEWSKI

headliners

THE MILLBROOK PRESS · BROOKFIELD, CONNECTICUT

Published by The Millbrook Press, Inc.
2 Old New Milford Road
Brookfield, CT   06804
www.millbrookpress.com

Library of Congress Cataloging-in-Publication Data
Andryszewski, Tricia, 1956-
Terrorism in America / Tricia Andryszewski.
p. cm. — (Headliners)
Summary: An account of the September 11 attacks in the United States,
with a discussion of the war on terrorism, anthrax attacks, and new
security measures put into place since that day.
Includes bibliographical references and index.
ISBN 0-7613-2803-3 (lib. binding)
1. Terrorism—United States—Juvenile literature. 2.
Terrorism—United States—History—Juvenile literature. 3.
Americans—Violence against—Foreign countries—Juvenile literature. 4.
September 11 Terrorist Attacks, 2001—Juvenile literature. [1.
Terrorism. 2. Political violence. 3. September 11 Terrorist Attacks,
2001. 4. War on Terrorism, 2001-] I. Title. II. Series.
HV6432 .A57 2002 363.3'2'0973—dc21   2001007801

Cover photographs courtesy of AP/Wide World Photos
Photographs courtesy of AP/Wide World Photos: pp. 1, 4, 6, 9, 14, 17, 29, 39, 44, 53;
Archive Photos: p. 11 (© Roz Payne); © Reuters NewMedia Inc./Corbis: p. 20 (top; bottom
right); TimePix: pp. 20 (bottom right © Ted Thai), 27, 37 (Reuters), 46 (© Pawel
Kopdzynski/Reuters); Corbis Sygma: p. 23 (© Jeffrey Markowitz); © Getty Images: p. 41
(Al Rai Al Aam)

CONTENTS

SEPTEMBER 11, 2001

Early on September 11, 2001, an ordinary Tuesday morning, thousands of workers were streaming into the two tall towers of New York City's World Trade Center and settling in for a day at their desks or shops.

At 8:48 A.M., a large passenger jet, full of thousands of gallons of fuel to fly it to California, plowed into the World Trade Center's 110-story north tower at about the 100th floor. The big building swallowed the plane, shuddered, and remained standing. A fireball erupted and black smoke billowed out of the building. Office workers who were blocked from exits by the intense heat of the burning jet fuel jumped to their deaths. One couple jumped holding hands. Thousands of other workers, on lower floors not yet burning, made their way to the building's stairways and began the long descent to the street below.

Only eighteen minutes later another large jet, also bound for California, rammed into the World Trade Center's other tall tower. At that moment, it became clear that this was no accident. It was an act of terrorism.

Thick black smoke filled the sky in lower Manhattan on Tuesday, September 11, 2001, shortly after terrorists crashed two passenger planes into the World Trade Center. Another plane crashed into the Pentagon, and a fourth crashed in rural Pennsylvania during the terrorist attack.

Police officers, firefighters, and other rescue workers rushed to the burning buildings to tend to the wounded and help people escape. Thousands upon thousands of people exited the twin towers, stepping aside in the stairways from time to time to allow the injured to pass them on their way down and firefighters to pass them on their way up.

Meanwhile, elsewhere, two other jetliners had been hijacked by terrorists with similar plans. One, at 9:40 A.M., crashed into the western side of the Pentagon, the U.S. Defense Department's headquarters outside Washington, D.C. The other, its hijackers apparently thwarted by heroic civilians on the plane, crashed into a field in south-central Pennsylvania at 10 A.M.

The World Trade Center continued to burn. Jet fuel burns hot—hot enough to soften the steel columns that keep skyscrapers standing up. At 9:59 A.M., the unthinkable happened: The south tower of the World Trade Center collapsed in a heap, grinding to incinerated dust thousands of people trapped inside.

"It can't be. It just can't be," one woman said, looking at the empty space where a moment ago the tower had stood. "Where did it go? Oh, lord, where did it go?" Half an hour later, the north tower, too, collapsed in a huge cloud of black smoke and pale ash.

All 265 passengers and crew on the four hijacked airplanes died that morning, including the planes' hijackers. At the Pentagon, 125 workers and visitors died. At the World Trade Center, nearly 3,000 were killed, including hundreds of rescue workers. It was by far the most deadly terrorist attack in U.S. history.

CHAPTER 1

TERRORISM IN AMERICA'S PAST

Terrorism is the use of violence, or the threat of violence, to frighten or intimidate and to move people to take actions that further the terrorists' goals. Terrorists may, for example, set off a bomb or hijack an airplane to convince the public that they are powerful and dangerous, to force a government or industry to meet a set of demands, or to provoke a government to undermine its legitimacy by undertaking unpopular security measures. Some groups or individuals use terrorist acts to force people to change their way of life in keeping with the terrorists' beliefs. Others try to topple a government and change a country's leadership. And some governments use terrorism to squelch their political opposition.

By spreading fears that nobody, anywhere, is safe, terrorists strike not only at their immediate victims but also at a much wider public. To add to this wider effect, many—but not all—terrorists claim credit for their violent actions, hoping that media coverage will spread their message.

The Ku Klux Klan

The Ku Klux Klan (KKK), the longest-running and best-known terrorist movement in the United States, first arose in 1865. At the end of the Civil War, Southern whites were forced to surren-

Members of the Ku Klux Klan in a parade in Tulsa, Oklahoma, on September 21, 1923.

der to the victorious North and to free their black slaves. Many white Southerners who refused to accept these changes joined together in a new organization—the Ku Klux Klan. Klansmen with white hoods hiding their faces threatened, harassed, robbed, assaulted, mutilated, raped, and murdered Southern blacks and destroyed their property. The Klan's intention was to terrorize the black population into meek submission and to re-establish many of the old conditions of slavery, even though the law said the former slaves were now free. When law and custom established a new system of racial segregation in the late 1800s, the Klan faded.

Decades later, in the 1920s, the Klan rose again. This time, the Klan's reach extended well beyond the Deep South into much of the rural Midwest and West. The Klan moved into politics, working to elect sympathetic mayors, governors, and even members of Congress. And, true to its roots, it also unleashed a wave of terrorist violence, not only against blacks but now also against Jews, Catholics, "foreigners," and even white women who exhibited too much independence.

In the late 1950s and early 1960s, Southern blacks and their white supporters demanded an end to racial segregation and full equality of opportunity for America's black citizens. Many whites opposed this civil rights movement, and a revived Ku Klux Klan was able to recruit thousands of members to fight it. Klan actions ranged from beating up peaceful protesters (often with the quiet approval of local police) to church bombings and dozens of lynchings. But the Klan failed to derail the civil rights movement. Since then, the KKK has never amounted to more than a tiny fringe movement.

New Movements

Beginning with the civil rights movement for racial equality, a wave of wide-ranging social change swept the United States in the 1960s and 1970s. Millions of mostly young Americans participated in civil rights demonstrations and protests against America's war in Vietnam. Later, environmental and women's and other movements, too, mobilized millions of Americans to press for change.

In 1968, emotions ran high and many protests became violent. Local as well as federal law enforcement agents used what many considered excessive force against protesters, peaceful and not. A violent, terrorist fringe, goaded by hard-line policing and dissatisfied with the pace of social change, spun off from the mass protest movements. In the years that followed, bombings and other acts of terrorism were committed by small groups of leftist "revolutionaries." The best known of these terrorists were the Black

A group of Black Panthers with their fists raised, as a sign of Black Power, at the Panther 21 trial, when twenty one leaders of the Black Panthers were tried and acquitted on charges of conspiracy in New York City in 1969.

Panthers and the Weather Underground. The Black Panthers wanted to incite a violent revolution on behalf of black Americans. The Weather Underground derived from the student antiwar protests of the 1960s and survived into the 1970s as a small network living "underground" (in hiding from the law) and occasionally committing terrorist acts in pursuit of a socialist revolution.

Fueled by the same kinds of social ferment and beginning at about the same time, a similar wave of leftist-revolutionary, antigovernment terrorist acts were committed by small groups in European and Latin American countries. While in the United States the revolutionary terrorists soon dwindled to a near-dormant handful of activists, in Europe they were very visibly active for much longer, striking against U.S. military targets as well as Europeans in the 1970s and 1980s. These small groups of terrorists shared resources with each other and had a common agenda—to destroy the political/economic/social order of the worlds' industrialized, capitalist nations (western Europe, Japan, and especially the United States) to pave the way for a new, socialist/communist world order.

Meanwhile, closer to home, Americans became a target of terrorists supporting Puerto Rican independence from the United States. The best-known terrorist group supporting Puerto Rican independence was the FALN, which was most active in the mid-1970s to mid-1980s. The FALN is believed to have been responsible for a December 1975 bombing at New York's LaGuardia Airport that killed twelve people.

In addition, the United States during the 1970s and 1980s became a secondary target of Latin American terrorists fighting governments supported by the United States. At that time, the United States was fighting a "Cold War" against communist Russia. The United States supported governments around the world that would take its side in this conflict, while the Russians did the same.

In Latin America and elsewhere, the United States gave military and financial aid to anticommunist governments, many of which brutally repressed their own people. Americans traveling to or living in these countries were sometimes killed by local terrorists opposing U.S. support for their repressive governments. Many of these governments fought back with state-sponsored terrorist campaigns of their own, apparently to frighten their citizens into submission to state authority. In the 1990s, since the end of the Cold War, this particular vicious cycle of terrorism against terrorism has mostly ended—but the memory of U.S. aid for repressive regimes lingers.

CHAPTER 2

FOREIGN TERRORISTS TARGET AMERICANS

If you had asked most Americans to define "terrorism" anytime from the late 1970s to the early 1990s, they'd have described a threat from shadowy foreigners against Americans traveling outside the United States. Again and again in those years, Americans abroad were taken hostage, threatened aboard hijacked airplanes, and often killed. No place was safe—Americans were murdered by terrorists in a U.S. embassy, in a German nightclub, even on board a cruise ship. This long run of top-of-the-news anti-American terrorism abroad began in earnest with the Iranian hostage crisis, in 1979.

The Iran Hostage Crisis

Iran in the 1970s was ruled by Mohammad Reza Shah Pahlavi. The shah for many years pursued plans to "modernize" Iran through more schooling of the mostly illiterate masses, more industry, and closer ties with the United States and the industrialized nations of Europe. The shah also used a brutal police force against his critics and enriched himself and his family and friends (as well as American oil companies) with money derived from Iran's huge supply of oil. As oil prices rose in the 1970s, the shah became fabulously rich—and the mostly poor people of Iran became more and more resentful.

One of the shah's most persistent critics was the ultraconservative Muslim religious leader Ayatollah Ruholla Khomeini. The ayatollah preached that the shah's program to modernize Iran was offensive to God. He said it was sinful, for example, for women to wear "immodest" American-style clothes. He also objected to giving Iranian children a secular, Western-style education (like what's offered in American public schools) instead of orthodox Muslim religious training. The shah and his corrupt government must be swept away, Khomeini told his followers, and replaced by a system run according to the laws and principles of his brand of Islam.

But the ayatollah's "holy war" wasn't directed at the shah only. Khomeini also told all who would listen that the shah was simply following the bad example of America—the "Great Satan," the central source of the moral corruption of modernization spreading throughout the world. The ayatollah urged his followers not only to make a revolution in Iran but also to attack America's influence—and Americans—around the world, all in the name of God.

The shah of Iran, Reza Pahlavi, and his wife, Empress Farah Diba, in Morocco in 1979, after they were forced to leave Iran by supporters of Ayatollah Khomeini, who took control of the government.

The ayatollah's message proved popular. In early 1979, the shah was forced to flee Iran, and a new government headed by Ayatollah Khomeini took power.

The new Iranian government claimed ownership of Iran's oil fields and industries, forced many of the shah's cronies to leave the country (or executed them), mandated a strict Islamic dress code, forbade American-style music and television, and began to put in place new Islamic legal and educational systems. Young people were to be educated to be soldiers for God—and the chief enemy was the United States.

On November 4, 1979, hundreds of armed Iranian students stormed the American embassy in Tehran. The embassy received no protection from the Iranian police, and the U.S. Marines on guard there were soon overwhelmed. The Iranians captured the building and took all fifty-three Americans there hostage. Americans at home watched on television, horrified, as hostages were paraded blindfolded in front of angry mobs and forced to make anti-American statements. After 250 days, one hostage was released. The rest were released in January 1981, after 444 days of captivity.

State-Sponsored Terrorism

From the rise of Ayatollah Khomeini to the present, in the Middle East and elsewhere in the Muslim world, militant Islam has infused nationalist movements with new energy and many new recruits willing to die—or kill—in a jihad, a "holy war" against non-Muslims. For example, militant Islam has worked its way into the ongoing Palestinian nationalist movement and its conflict with Israel. In the 1980s, U.S. citizens were frequent victims of terrorists affiliated with this re-energized movement, terrorists who hate America both as a friend of Israel and as an enemy of their kind of totalitarian Islam.

But militant Islam hasn't been the only institution supporting terrorist acts against Americans abroad in recent years. Terrorists have been encouraged, financed, sheltered, and in many cases actively sponsored or hired by certain nations. The leaders of these nations have for various reasons—from politics within their borders to conflicts with other nations—seen terrorism as a worthwhile tool.

State-sponsored terrorism isn't new. The very word "terrorism" comes from the Reign of Terror in France in the 1790s, when the revolutionary Robespierre and his government used executions by guillotine and other well-publicized violence to terrorize their fellow citizens into accepting their control over the country.

Most of the recent state sponsors of terrorism have been in the Middle East and North Africa. Iran, Iraq, Libya, Syria, Sudan, Afghanistan, and other so-called rogue states have provided military protection and safe havens for terrorists as well as money for terrorist activities, paying for equipment, living and travel expenses, and training and testing facilities.

Lockerbie

In April 1986, terrorists sponsored by Libya bombed a Berlin nightclub popular with U.S. servicemen, perhaps in retaliation for U.S. restrictions on travel by Libyans in the United States. (Libya, a known sponsor of terrorism, had poor relations with the United States, and the U.S. government had asserted that Libyans in America posed a terrorist threat.) Two Americans and a Turkish woman were killed in the nightclub bombing and 230 people were wounded, many of them Americans.

In response, the United States sent military jets to bomb targets in Libya. At least 15 people were killed, including one of Libyan leader Muammar al-Qaddafi's children.

Libya's response was a long time coming. In December 1988, a bomb was planted aboard a large passenger jet bound for New York from London. Pan Am Flight 103 blew up over Lockerbie,

La Belle nightclub in Berlin, Germany, after a bombing in
April 1986 that was ordered by Libya.

Scotland, instantly killing all 259 aboard, many of them Americans. Eleven more people died when the wreckage hit a row of houses on the ground.

After a long investigation, U.S. officials concluded that the bomb had been built by two Libyan agents, then placed on board a London-bound flight in Frankfurt, West Germany. Following directions on luggage-labeling tags stolen by the Libyans, the suitcase containing the bomb was transferred to Pan Am Flight 103 in London. Despite demands by the United States and other nations that the terrorists be brought to justice, Libya for years protected them. When they were finally put on trial, at an international court in the Netherlands, one was convicted and one was set free in February 2001.

After Lockerbie

In December 1988, Palestinian leader Yasir Arafat announced that he and his Palestine Liberation Organization would no longer use or support terrorism in their struggle with Israel. Terrorist attacks against Americans outside Israel diminished. However, other Arab terrorists continued to commit suicide bombings and other terrorist attacks inside Israel that claimed the lives of Americans as well as Israelis.

Around the time of the 1991 Persian Gulf war against Iraq, American concerns about terrorism increased. Iraq was a known sponsor of terrorism, and Americans feared that since Iraqi leader Saddam Hussein wouldn't win against U.S. troops on the battlefield, he might retaliate through acts of terror against U.S. citizens. Fortunately, special antiterrorist security at U.S. airports, a policy of expelling people associated with Saddam from the United States and various allied nations, the wartime international trade embargo against Iraq, and the wartime bombing of Iraq apparently disrupted Iraq's ability to launch terrorist strikes against Americans—at least for a while.

CHAPTER 3

TERROR COMES TO AMERICA
THE 1993 WORLD TRADE CENTER BOMBING

The 1993 bombing of the World Trade Center in New York City changed the way Americans saw terrorism. Terrorism for many years had been seen as something taking place outside the United States. At the World Trade Center, the terrorists brought their foreign conflicts and terrorist weapons to America.

A Massive Truck Bomb— and a Wider Conspiracy

On February 26, 1993, a terrible explosion ripped through a parking garage underneath the World Trade Center in New York City. It was just after noon on a workday, and the buildings were full of tens of thousands of workers and visitors. Smoke from the explosion and resulting fires billowed up through the towers. Six people died. More than a thousand were injured, mostly from inhaling smoke.

Investigators set to work to find out what had caused the explosion. Carefully sifting through tons of debris, they soon had a very lucky break: They found bits of a yellow rental van big enough to have held the explosives for such a blast. The van was traced to a young man named Mohammed A. Salameh, a Jordanian-born Palestinian living in Jersey City, New Jersey. On

A massive crater in the parking garage under the World Trade Center, where a bomb exploded on February 26, 1993, killing six and injuring more than a thousand.

Sheik Omar Abdel Rahman, a Muslim cleric whose followers—including Mohammed Salameh, right, planned the 1993 WTC bombing.

March 4, police arrested Salameh. Later, they found various bomb-making tools and related evidence at Salameh's apartment.

Salameh hadn't acted alone. He and more than a dozen fellow conspirators were eventually charged not only in connection with the World Trade Center bombing but also with plotting a wider terrorist bombing and assassination campaign directed at targets in the New York area and in Egypt. The intention of the planned campaign was to force the United States to stop supporting the governments of Israel and Egypt, which, according to the conspirators' spiritual leader, were enemies of Islam.

The conspirators were all followers of Sheik Omar Abdel Rahman, a radical Muslim cleric who came to the United States from Egypt in 1990. In November of that year, one of Abdel Rahman's followers, El Sayyid A. Nosair, was arrested for the fatal shooting of the militant Jewish extremist Rabbi Meir Kahane at an appearance in New York. In 1991, Nosair was convicted on weapons charges related to the Kahane assassination.

Around this time, according to a government informer, Abdel Rahman and the other conspirators discussed plots to free Nosair from prison and to assassinate Egyptian president Hosni Mubarak. But that was only the beginning. Over the next couple of years, they worked on plans to bomb such New York landmarks as the Holland and Lincoln tunnels, the New York Federal Building, and the United Nations headquarters.

The Conspirators Are Brought to Justice

In September 1993, Mohammed Salameh and three other followers of Abdel Rahman went on trial for carrying out the World Trade Center bombing. Prosecutors demonstrated that the defendants had bought bomb chemicals and taken them to a rented space in New Jersey. The prosecutors also showed that a letter claiming responsibility for the bombing had been produced on a computer tied to one of the four.

In March 1994, the jury found all four guilty. But the case wasn't closed. At least two additional conspirators—including the bombing's alleged "mastermind," Ramzi Ahmed Yousef—had gone overseas right after the bombing and remained free.

In 1995, the federal government brought Abdel Rahman and nine codefendants to trial on conspiracy charges related to the wider terrorist plot, which prosecutors called a "war of urban terrorism." (An additional conspirator pleaded guilty to lesser charges in a separate trial.) In October, all of the ten codefendants were found guilty, most on conspiracy and attempted bombing charges. Abdel Rahman was convicted of leading the terrorist conspiracy. Nosair was found guilty of the murder of Meir Kahane, but he and his cousin Ibrahim El-Gabrowny were found not guilty of direct involvement in the conspiracy to blow up New York landmarks. In January 1996, Abdel Rahman was sentenced to life in prison. His associates drew prison sentences ranging from twenty-five years to life.

Ramzi Yousef

In February 1995, Ramzi Yousef was arrested in Pakistan and flown to New York to be tried for the 1993 World Trade Center bombing. Flying into New York, an FBI agent guarding Yousef loosened his blindfold and pointed toward the World Trade Center's twin towers. "Look down there," he said. "They're still standing."

"They wouldn't be," Yousef responded, "if I had enough money and explosives."

Investigators accused Yousef of buying the chemicals used to make the bomb and participating in the actual placement of the bomb at the World Trade Center. Yousef had first arrived in the

$2,000,000

REWARD

At approximately 12 noon on February 26, 1993, a massive explosion rocked the World Trade Center in New York City, causing millions of dollars in damage. The terrorists who bombed the World Trade Center murdered six innocent people, injured over 1,000 others, and left terrified school children trapped for hours in smoke filled elevators.

Following the bombing, law enforcement officials obtained evidence which led to the indictments and arrests of several suspected terrorists involved in the bombing. RAMZI AHMED YOUSEF, one of those indicted, fled the United States immediately after the bombing to avoid arrest. YOUSEF is now a fugitive from justice. YOUSEF was born in Iraq or Kuwait, possesses Iraqi and Pakistani passports, and also claims to be a citizen of the United Arab Emirates. Because of the nature of the crimes for which he is charged, YOUSEF should be considered armed and extremely dangerous.

The United States Department of State is offering a reward of up to $2,000,000 for information leading to the apprehension and prosecution of YOUSEF. If you have information about YOUSEF or the World Trade Center bombing, contact the authorities, or the nearest U.S. embassy or consulate. In the United States, call your local office of the Federal Bureau of Investigation or 1-800-HEROES1, or write to:

HEROES
Post Office Box 96781
Washington, D.C. 20090 – 6781
U.S.A.

RAMZI AHMED YOUSEF

DESCRIPTION

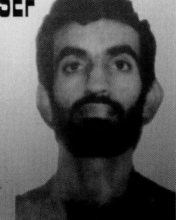

DATE OF BIRTH:	May 20, 1967 and/or April 27, 1968
PLACE OF BIRTH:	Iraq, Kuwait, or United Arab Emirates
HEIGHT:	6'
WEIGHT:	180 pounds
BUILD:	medium
HAIR:	brown
EYES:	brown
COMPLEXION:	olive
SEX:	male
RACE:	white
CHARACTERISTICS:	sometimes is clean shaven
ALIASES:	Ramzi A. Yousef, Ramzi Ahmad Yousef, Ramzi Yousef, Ramzi Yousef Ahmad, Ramzi Yousef Ahmed, Rasheed Yousef, Rashid Rashid, Rashed, Kamal Ibraham, Kamal Abraham, Abraham Kamal, Muhammad Azan, Khurram Khan, Abdul Basit.

A reward poster showing Ramzi Ahmed Yousef, who was finally arrested in 1995.

United States in 1992, requesting political asylum. While immigration authorities were processing his case, investigators said, Yousef was planning and carrying out the World Trade Center bombing. Yousef was convicted of this in 1997.

First, however, Ramzi Yousef and two other men were put on trial for yet another terrorist scheme: a plot to bomb as many as a dozen U.S. airliners in midair over the Pacific Ocean. (The plot was foiled when bomb-making facilities were discovered in the Philippines.) On September 5, 1996, Yousef and his two coconspirators were convicted of all charges against them in the airline bombing plot.

CHAPTER 4

HOMEGROWN TERRORISM

In the early 1980s, the United States experienced a wave of terrorist violence committed by various small groups operating inside its own borders. Much as the KKK arose in response to the freeing of slaves, these groups were reacting to wide-ranging changes in American society begun in the 1960s, especially to expanded freedoms and opportunities for blacks and women. The federal government poured money and personnel into a sustained crackdown on these groups. The FBI and other law enforcement agencies thoroughly and persistently investigated each act of terrorism, prosecuted the perpetrators, and especially sought out and prosecuted terrorist leaders.

Terrorists of the 1980s

In the early 1980s, a loosely linked network of racist American terrorists gathered strength and readied themselves for action. These terrorists considered themselves at war with the U.S. government and were often affiliated with the quasi-religious white supremacist Christian Identity movement, which holds that white "Aryans," not Jews, are God's "chosen people" and that a worldwide racial "holy war" is imminent.

In 1983, several dozen Ku Klux Klansmen, white racist "survivalists," and neo-Nazis banded together in a group they called the Order. (Survivalists, typically Christian Identity believers, think that Armageddon—the end of the world—is near and that white Christians should prepare to defend themselves against the forces of Satan, typically by holing up with their families in remote, heavily fortified homesteads. Neo-Nazis believe that Adolf Hitler's plans for Nazi Germany in the 1930s and 1940s are a blueprint for how the world ought to be run.) The members of the Order shared a passionate belief in Christian Identity and a conviction that fomenting a race war/revolution in America was the work of God. Inspired by *The Turner Diaries*, a neo-Nazi novel about race war, Order members ran a successful counterfeiting operation and committed a series of murders and robberies in 1983 and 1984, including the execution of the liberal, Jewish, Denver-based radio talk-show host Alan Berg in June 1984.

By the end of the 1980s, law enforcement officials had successfully shut the Order down and forced other white racist terrorist groups to disband or go underground. Fugitive Order leader Robert Mathews was killed when his own stockpile of ammunition caught fire during a confrontation with police; other Order members were sentenced to long prison terms.

But this was by no means the end of the Order's influence. A wide range of white supremacists came to view Mathews as a martyr and the imprisoned Order members as "prisoners of war." Many also came to view the U.S. government as the Order's chief enemy.

During the time the Order was active, other terrorists bombed and vandalized hundreds of medical facilities in the United States, motivated by antiabortion fervor. Antiabortion arson and bombing attacks began in the 1970s and increased in the 1980s. In 1989, the first of several waves of letters falsely claiming to be laced with potentially deadly anthrax bacteria was mailed to abortion clinics around the country. In the 1990s, the violence came to include direct physical attacks on medical personnel. Several people who worked at health care clinics that provide abortions have been murdered.

Another set of terrorists, first noted nationally in the late 1980s, supported environmental goals and animal rights. Although Earth First! and the Animal Liberation Front are the best-known of these groups associated with these causes, most terrorist acts seem to have been committed by unknown individuals or cells, small groups that share the goals of a broader movement but act in isolation. Most acts of pro-environmental and animal rights terrorism have destroyed property and not targeted people.

Terrorism can sometimes be hard to distinguish from the acts of lone fanatics. Surprisingly, America's longest-running terrorism mystery turned out to be the work of one such unique loner—the Unabomber, a shadowy assassin responsible for a series of sixteen bombing incidents directed mostly against universities and airlines. Between 1978 and 1995, three people were killed and twenty-three injured in these attacks. In April 1996, law enforcement officials finally arrested the Unabomber: Theodore J. Kaczynski, a former professor with a hatred of modern technology-based society who was then living in a remote part of Montana. Convicted in 1998, Kaczynski is now serving a life sentence in prison.

The cover of *Time* magazine on April 15, 1996, showing the Unabomber, Ted Kaczynski, a few weeks after he was finally apprehended in his cabin in a remote part of Montana.

The Militia Movement

In the early 1990s, experts on hate groups and terrorism in the United States began to notice a thickening climate of hatred with frightening terrorist potential in the antigovernment militia movement. As had been the case with the KKK in its early days, support for this new movement was widespread and rooted in a reaction against social change. Many Americans felt threatened by the greater opportunities and freedoms extended to women and minorities in recent years and by American society's increased acceptance of diversity and tolerance of lifestyles and behaviors many considered immoral. Most of those who supported the militia movement sought a safe haven for themselves and their families and a mutual defense against what they saw as an increasingly hostile mainstream America. A few were ready to use this base of defense-oriented support to mount violent attacks.

Militia movement supporters in the early 1990s favored conspiracy theories invoking fears of a world government dominated by Jews and nonwhites. They opposed gun control and believed that they were being persecuted by an increasingly tyrannical federal government. Violent white supremacists who viewed the U.S. government as their chief enemy recruited and spread their propaganda among militia members. As a result, many of those affiliated with the militia movement also became involved with racist hate groups, many or perhaps most accepted the notion of white supremacy, and many believed in Christian Identity ideology.

Militia members and their supporters came from diverse backgrounds, and militia activities varied from group to group. Some militia-oriented extremists were loners or only loosely affiliated with others who shared their beliefs. Others, organized into groups, concentrated on stockpiling weapons and conducting regular military training in anticipation of a confrontation with the government. Still others produced and distributed newsletters, books, videos, and other propaganda.

Many militia extremists felt their antigovernment resolve harden in response to three key events:

• **_Ruby Ridge:_** a shootout between federal officials and white separatist/survivalist Randy Weaver in 1992 at Weaver's isolated home in Ruby Ridge, Idaho, resulting in the death of Weaver's fourteen-year-old son and unarmed wife.

Randy Weaver's home on Ruby Ridge near Naples, Idaho, where confiscated guns and ammunition were laid out following the shooting of his wife and son by federal agents.

- **Waco:** a long siege in 1993 by federal agents at the Branch Davidian complex in Waco, Texas, ending in an attack on the complex by federal law enforcement agents and a fire that killed dozens inside. Militia extremists viewed both Ruby Ridge and Waco as examples of a violently oppressive federal government run amok.

- **Federal gun-control legislation** signed into law in 1993 and 1994, specifically the "Brady bill" (requiring a waiting period to allow background checks before any handgun purchase) and the "assault weapons ban" (a ten-year ban on the sale of certain kinds of semiautomatic guns and ammunition). Militia extremists as well as more mainstream gun-rights advocates believed that arming oneself against potential government tyranny is an essential civil right and that government gun control measures infringe upon that right.

While these issues were drawing more and more angry individuals into the militia movement, hate-group leaders were promoting a special strategy for mobilizing the movement's hard core for terrorist action. In 1992, Louis Beam, a former Klansman who had written some of the most militant white supremacist propaganda of the 1980s, published an article called "Leaderless Resistance"—a blueprint for creating a network of independent terrorist cells—that became a popular piece of literature on the militia circuit.

As Beam describes it, leaderless resistance, or "phantom cell" organization

> does not have any central control or direction. . . . All individuals and groups operate independently of each other, and never report to a central headquarters or single leader for direction or instruction. . . . Organs of information distribution such as newspapers, leaflets, computers, etc., which are widely available to all, keep each person

informed of events, allowing for a planned response that will take many variations. No one need issue an order to anyone. Those idealists truly committed to the cause of freedom will act when they feel the time is ripe, or will take their cue from others who precede them. . . . It goes almost without saying that Leaderless Resistance leads to very small or even one-man cells of resistance [that present] no single opportunity for the Federals to destroy a significant portion of the resistance.

Oklahoma City

In the early 1990s, a militia movement activist named Timothy McVeigh steeped himself in extremist literature. McVeigh was almost certainly familiar with the concept of leaderless resistance, and he had expressed outrage about gun control and about the federal government's conduct at Waco. On Wednesday, April 19, 1995, McVeigh bombed the federal building in Oklahoma City, killing 168 people, including 19 children.

The Oklahoma City bombing shocked the American public. At that time, it was the deadliest terrorist attack ever committed on U.S. soil, and it put terrorism on the front pages of American newspapers day after day after day.

Within hours after the Oklahoma City explosion, investigators concluded that it had been caused by hundreds of pounds of explosives hidden in a car or truck. They began seeking two suspects—young men resembling white American GIs, not Islamic "holy warriors" as many Americans had immediately thought likely. The men had rented a truck believed to have been loaded with the explosives and left it at the federal building. On Friday, federal law enforcement authorities announced that one of these men, Timothy James McVeigh, was under arrest.

McVeigh, age 27, a native of suburban Buffalo, New York, had served in the army in the Persian Gulf war. Attracted to the militia movement, he had networked with militia activists and sympathizers in the Midwest and West. Law enforcement officials building the case against McVeigh believed that militia movement ideology motivated the bombing.

Soon after McVeigh's arrest, a friend of his, Terry Lynn Nichols, turned himself in for questioning. On May 10, Terry Nichols was formally charged with participating in the Oklahoma City bombing. Both McVeigh and Nichols pleaded not guilty.

In June 1997, a jury unanimously found McVeigh guilty on all counts—from conspiracy to use of a weapon of mass destruction to murder—and sentenced him to death. Nichols, in a separate trial, was convicted of conspiracy and involuntary manslaughter but acquitted of murder. He was sentenced to life in prison. Timothy McVeigh was executed by lethal injection in June 2001.

The Antiabortion/Militia Connection

The militant wing of the antiabortion movement predates the militia movement, but to some extent they overlapped and networked in the 1990s. Militia leaders were often arrested at antiabortion protests, and individuals active in the militia movement have been convicted of conspiring to bomb abortion clinics. Radical elements of both the militia movement and the antiabortion movement have seen themselves as being literally at war with a government that sanctions and supports what they believe are fundamentally immoral values.

Antiabortion terrorists don't usually publicly take "credit" for their actions. Often the only clues indicating that separate clinic bombings or other acts of terror might have a common perpetrator are in the physical evidence, at the bomb site, of how the bombs were made and with what ingredients. Because such evidence is usually inconclusive, investigators can spend years chasing up blind alleys in search of an elusive bomber or team of terrorists.

For example, in July 1996 a pipe bomb exploded during a free rock concert at a crowded park in Atlanta, Georgia, near the Olympic Games being held there, killing one person and injuring 111. No one credibly claimed responsibility for the bombing. For months thereafter, investigators and the press hounded the wrong suspect, the innocent security guard who had first noticed the knapsack containing the bomb at the park. Eventually, though, subsequent bombings revealed an antiabortion/militia connection.

In June 1997, law enforcement officials announced that they were "all but positive" that one person or small group had planted bombs earlier that year at an abortion clinic and at a nightclub catering to lesbians, both in Atlanta—and that the officials had "increasing confidence" that these bombings were linked to the Olympic bombing. The officials released excerpts from letters sent to news organizations after the nightclub and clinic bombings. These letters, laced with antiabortion, antihomosexual, and antigovernment vitriol, claimed that the bombings had been "carried out by units of the Army of God." (For many years, antiabortion terrorists scattered across the country have referred to themselves as being part of an "Army of God," although it's not clear how, if at all, these diverse terrorist cells and individuals have been linked.

Was the Olympic bombing part of a wider campaign by a terrorist group that, for whatever reasons, chose not to claim responsibility? Or was it the work of a lone lunatic, like the Unabomber? At a time when "leaderless resistance" by loners or very small groups acting independently but devoted to a wider movement had become a preferred organizing strategy for terrorists, perhaps this distinction didn't much matter.

CHAPTER 5
NEW ATTACKS ON AMERICANS ABROAD

While militia-related and other homegrown terrorism played out in the United States, foreign terrorists continued to attack Americans abroad. The most deadly of these attacks have been linked to al-Qaeda, the Islamic revolutionary terrorist network associated with a wealthy Saudi fanatic, Osama bin Laden:

- In October 1993, American soldiers participating in a United Nations peacemaking mission in Somalia were ambushed, with eighteen killed. U.S. investigators later determined that the Somalis who ambushed the American soldiers were trained and assisted by al-Qaeda.

- In 1995, a bomb killed four Americans working in Saudi Arabia. The killers, who confessed to the crime, said they had never met bin Laden and were not working for him but were inspired by him.

- In June 1996, a truck bomb killed nineteen U.S. servicemen at their quarters in Dhahran, Saudi Arabia.

- In August 1998, truck bombs exploded ten minutes apart at U.S. embassies in Nairobi, Kenya, and Dar es Salaam, Tanzania, killing 223 and injuring more than 5,500. Two weeks after the bombings, the United States launched cruise missile attacks on a camp in Afghanistan that bin Laden was believed to be visiting (the attack missed him by perhaps as little as an hour) and on a pharmaceutical plant in Sudan mistakenly believed to be involved in chemical weapons production for bin Laden's network. In 2001, four individuals associated with bin Laden and al-Qaeda were convicted in New York in connection with the embassy bombings; at least one had ties both to Osama bin Laden and to the 1993 World Trade Center bombers, and another told prosecutors that he had trained Islamic militants in Somalia.

- Law enforcement foiled a plot by al-Qaeda members to blow up targets in Jordan around the turn of the millennium, January 1, 2000, aiming to kill U.S. and Israeli tourists. A second, related attack to take place at the Los Angeles airport was also discovered in time to avert it.
- In October 2000, terrorists linked to al-Qaeda blew up a small boat filled with explosives alongside the *U.S.S. Cole*, a Navy warship docked for refueling in the port of Aden, Yemen. Nineteen U.S. sailors died and thirty-nine were wounded.

Who Is Osama bin Laden?

Born in 1957 in Saudi Arabia, Osama bin Laden is one of fifty-two children of the several wives of a businessman born in Yemen. Osama bin Laden is his mother's only child. His father became vastly wealthy through contracts for government-sponsored construction work in Saudi Arabia. When he died in 1968, young Osama inherited a fortune variously estimated at $20 million to $80 million or perhaps as high as $300 million. Osama bin Laden attended college in Saudi Arabia and received a degree in civil engineering in 1979.

Bin Laden became intensely, radically religious in the late 1970s. He himself has attributed this to three events: 1) the U.S.-brokered peace accord between Israel and Egypt, which angered him because he does not think Jews should govern any part of the Muslim holy lands of the Middle East; 2) the Islamic revolution in Iran, which demonstrated that an uncompromising government based entirely on a radically strict interpretation of Islam could be established; and especially 3) the invasion of Muslim Afghanistan by communist Russia in 1979—an attack on Islam by atheists, in bin Laden's view.

In the early 1980s, bin Laden busied himself raising money to fight the Russians in Afghanistan. In 1984 he moved to Peshawar, Pakistan, near the Afghanistan border. There he dispensed charitable aid and built training camps for guerrillas fighting the Russians. His money and generosity made many friends for him in Afghanistan and elsewhere in the world among Muslims outraged by the Russian occupation there.

Among those friends were fellow Arabs, Islamic militants affiliated with Egyptian Islamic Jihad, a terrorist group responsible for the 1981 assassination of Egypt's President Anwar Sadat. Together, in 1988, bin Laden and the Egyptian terrorists formed al-Qaeda, "The Base," an international coalition of various like-minded groups and individuals that would carry the Muslim militants' fight against non-Muslim Russian "infidels" in Afghanistan to other parts of the world, wherever non-Muslims ruled over Muslims.

After the defeated Russians finally left Afghanistan in 1989, bin Laden and his al-Qaeda associates poured money into training camps and guest houses for Islamic militants fighting this new, worldwide jihad, or holy war. (Ramzi Yousef, mastermind of the 1993 World Trade Center bombing, stayed at one of these guest houses, in Pakistan. The leader of the millennium plot in Jordan trained in Afghanistan in the early 1990s.)

Bin Laden himself returned to Saudi Arabia. In 1990, during the Persian Gulf war against Iraq, the Saudi government invited the United States to send troops to Saudi Arabia. Since then, enraged that "infidel" American troops are stationed in Saudi Arabia, the holy land where the Prophet Muhammad was born, bin Laden has made the United States his chief target.

Osama bin Laden, the leader behind some of the most horrific terrorist attacks on Americans both at home and abroad in the last decade, has called for Muslims everywhere to kill Americans.

Caught smuggling weapons, bin Laden was expelled from Saudi Arabia in 1991, and his Saudi citizenship was later revoked. He settled in Sudan, where an Islamic government had recently taken over. Pressured by the United States, in 1996 Sudan expelled bin Laden. He returned to Afghanistan, where Islamic revolutionaries known as the Taliban were taking control of the country after years of war and chaos. Bin Laden supported the Taliban and in return was given a safe haven for himself, for his three wives and fifteen children, and for al-Qaeda.

In August 1996, Osama bin Laden publicly declared a "holy war" against the United States and urged attacks on U.S. soldiers. A year and a half later, in February 1998, he expanded the war, declaring that U.S. civilians as well as soldiers should be killed, anywhere in the world: "To kill Americans and their allies, both civil and military, is an individual duty of every Muslim who is able." Around this time, al-Qaeda merged with several other Islamic militant organizations. This dramatically extended al-Qaeda's reach, establishing it as a sort of franchiser for locally launched terrorist operations around the world. The U.S. embassy and *Cole* bombings, the failed millennium plot, and the September 11 attacks all appear to have been carried out by largely independent cells with financial and technical support from al-Qaeda but not much command and control. As with "leaderless resistance" organization among U.S. hate groups, this pattern has made it difficult for law enforcement to pin responsibility on terrorists beyond the local cells.

In a videotaped message made public in the summer of 2001, bin Laden made clear that he and al-Qaeda were aiming ultimately to destroy the United States. "With small capabilities, and with our faith," he said, "we can defeat the greatest military power of modern times. America is much weaker than it appears." Ominously, he urged his followers to become martyrs in this battle against America: "You will not die needlessly. Your lives are in the hands of God."

After the September 11, 2001, attack on the Pentagon in Washington, D.C., and the World Trade Center in New York City, all of America knew who Osama bin Laden was and what he looked like.

As a security measure, bin Laden moved around a lot, rarely sleeping more than two nights in the same place. He also avoided telephones and other electronic communications and instead conveyed information face to face. He did, however, reportedly telephone his mother in Lebanon on September 10, 2001, and tell her that "something big" was about to happen that would make it impossible for him to call her again "for a long time."

al-Qaeda

Bin Laden and al-Qaeda's key accomplishment has been making alliances among diverse Islamic terrorist organizations in many countries, enabling them to stop fighting among themselves and instead share information and other resources to maximum effect. As with U.S. terrorists, al-Qaeda also has exploited the sympathy of large numbers of people who feel threatened by social change—in this case Muslims in traditional societies at odds with the values of modern, liberal, aggressively market-driven America. By 2001, al-Qaeda had thousands of agents operating in dozens of countries. It has been financed partly by Osama bin Laden's personal fortune, partly by affiliated business enterprises, and partly by contributions.

Here's how al-Qaeda makes terrorist acts against America happen:

- Its members recruit volunteers willing to become martyrs for the cause.
- It provides training, both in the skills and knowledge needed to commit terrorist acts and in ideology intended to reinforce the recruits' willingness to be martyrs. At least 11,000 individuals have been trained in al-Qaeda's camps in Afghanistan since 1996, perhaps 3,000 as would-be martyrs, 8,000 as support personnel.

Terrorists training in an al-Qaeda camp.

- It plants these trained volunteers around the world, quietly, often years before they will commit their acts of terror.
- It supports these planted "sleepers" by supplying money, forged documents, and logistical information.
- It favors small, independent groups of operatives, similar to the "leaderless resistance" cells favored by antigovernment militants in the United States in the 1990s. Individual groups have much freedom in the choice and execution of their missions, and contacts with the network beyond the group are careful and few. If investigators break up one group, the rest of the network remains largely intact.
- It prepares each operation with meticulous care, taking several years if necessary, seeking to wreak maximum havoc with miminum expense. The 1998 embassy bombings were perhaps five years in the planning. The September 11, 2001, attacks were planned for about two years.

- Targets are chosen and actions planned that will attract extensive media coverage. Part of that coverage has featured bin Laden and his associates denying responsibility for attacks while heaping praise upon the perpetrators and encouraging others to follow their example.
- Many of al-Qaeda's operations are planned in pairs. The 1993 World Trade Center bombing was to be followed by another attack on New York area landmarks; the foiled millennium plot was to come in two waves. After the devastating September 11 hijackings, antiterrorism experts scrambled to discover what might come next.

CHAPTER 6

AFTER SEPTEMBER 11

Midday on Tuesday, September 11, 2001, an enormous heap of dust and twisted steel and crushed concrete—two million cubic yards of debris piled eight to nine stories high—covered the place where the twin towers of the World Trade Center had collapsed. The ruins creaked and moaned beneath the feet of rescuers searching for survivors. That day, only three people were found buried alive in the ruins. On Wednesday, two more were found. After that, no more. The site continued to smolder for months while emergency workers carted wreckage away.

Day by day, normal activities resumed around the United States. Airplanes grounded when the hijackings were first discovered began to fly again. Most of the Pentagon, the undamaged parts, reopened and government workers returned to work. On Monday, September 17, a few dozen yards from the World Trade Center, the New York Stock Exchange opened for business for the first time since the hijackings. The price of stocks fell sharply, then stabilized. The American economy, faltering for much of the previous year, slid into recession but didn't crash.

Meanwhile, investigators started to piece together the story of the hijacking plot. They learned that on the morning of September 11, teams of four or five terrorists, all or most of them from the Middle East, had boarded four planes that took off within minutes of each other from airports outside Boston, Newark,

An aerial view of lower Manhattan taken after September 11, 2001, showing the destruction after the terrorist attack.

and Washington. Using such crude weapons as box cutters, the hijackers killed or disabled crew members, took control of the planes, and aimed them at their targets. The hijackings had been planned for perhaps two years, and the nineteen hijackers were presumably helped by a network of supporters. Law enforcement officials immediately began looking for these supporters and indeed for anyone who might have information about the hijackers or the plot.

Within hours after the hijackings, counterterrorism officials intercepted communications indicating that Osama bin Laden's al-Qaeda organization was responsible for the attack. Afghanistan's Taliban regime immediately condemned the hijackings and said that bin Laden, their "guest," was not involved. Bin Laden himself denied responsibility but praised the hijackers.

Immediately after the September 11 attacks, Secretary of State Colin Powell and other U.S. diplomats began building an international coalition to respond. Secretary Powell promised to present the world with evidence linking Osama bin Laden and al-Qaeda to the attacks and asked all nations to help in the fight against international terrorism. The nature of that help would vary, from seizing bank accounts and other assets used to fund terrorism, to providing secret information on suspected terrorists, to supporting or participating in military operations against bin Laden in Afghanistan.

All fifteen members of the NATO (North Atlantic Treaty Organization) alliance promised their support. Russia, too, formerly NATO's adversary, promised to cooperate. Other nations, including those not usually friendly to the United States, were pressed to join the coalition as well. Nations controlled by Muslims, especially, were sought out, in order to reassure Muslims everywhere that the war against terrorism was not a war against Islam. Muslim and non-Muslim nations around the world condemned the September 11 attacks, and most moved toward cooperation with the effort to suppress al-Qaeda.

A key ally in the war against terrorism would be Pakistan, the foremost sponsor of the Taliban regime in neighboring Afghanistan. Pakistan, deep in debt, needed America's economic help. Its leader, General Pervez Musharraf, faced opposition from local militants who wanted a Taliban-style Islamic government in Pakistan, nearly all of whose citizens are Muslim. U.S. assistance could strengthen Musharraf's hand against the Islamic militants. On the other hand, any help he might give the United States in attacks on Afghanistan could backfire by enraging the militants, encouraging them to overthrow his government.

Reluctantly, Pakistan decided to cooperate with the United States. It began by mediating a persistent effort to persuade the

Taliban to hand Osama bin Laden over for trial. Pakistan also planned to offer other assistance to the United States and its allies if war began—sharing Pakistani military intelligence, cutting off Taliban supply lines, allowing U.S. and other allied bombers to fly over Pakistan en route to targets in Afghanistan. In return for Pakistan's cooperation, the United States began to organize substantial economic aid.

After weeks of hesitation, the Taliban finally refused to hand over bin Laden. U.S. bombers and other military aircraft and aircraft carriers moved within striking distance of Afghanistan. On October 6, U.S. President George W. Bush publicly told the Taliban that "full warning has been given, and time is running out."

By then it was clear that the war against terrorism would start with a military campaign against bin Laden and his associates and supporters in Afghanistan. A broader attack on international terrorists and their supporters would follow—but the nature and scope of that broader attack were far from clear. What, exactly, would the United States and its allies aim at in the wider war? Would the target be limited to al-Qaeda terrorists and their supporters in other countries? Would Iraq, a long-time sponsor of terrorism, be targeted even if it wasn't directly involved in the September 11 attacks? What

The leader of Pakistan, Pervez Musharraf, on a visit to New Delhi, India, in July 2001.

about other nations known to support terrorism or to harbor al-Qaeda terrorists, such as Iran, North Korea, and Somalia, or nations where al-Qaeda maintained operations against the will of the government, such as the Philippines? Widening the target would weaken the antiterrorism coalition. Many states, especially Arab states, would likely refuse to go beyond the initial target of bin Laden and al-Qaeda.

On October 7, U.S. and British warplanes began bombing Afghanistan. (At the same time, cargo planes began dropping packages of food for Afghan civilians, whose supply sources had been disrupted not only by war but also by several years of drought. Millions would need food and other humanitarian aid during the oncoming winter.) The bombing campaign soon knocked out what little infrastructure al-Qaeda and the Taliban commanded—training camps, air fields, and other facilities. As the enemy was dispersed and divided, U.S. and allied special military forces on the ground worked with local anti-Taliban forces to hunt down Osama bin Laden and his supporters, break up Taliban control of the country, and set the stage for a new Afghani government that would not support terrorism.

In early December, diverse anti-Taliban Afghanis meeting under U.N. sponsorship agreed to form a temporary government for Afghanistan. By then, the Taliban had already lost control of most of the country, including Kabul, the capital city. On December 7, Taliban forces abandoned Kandahar, the last city they held, and Taliban government of Afghanistan ended. However, many al-Qaeda fighters eluded capture and Taliban leader Mullah Mohammed Omar and Osama bin Laden remained at large.

Nuclear, Chemical, and Biological Weapons

By the time the bombing started in Afghanistan, Americans were alert to a new terror threat—anthrax.

Nuclear, chemical, and biological weapons are horrifying. The idea that terrorists might use such weapons has worried counterterrorism officials for many years. Fortunately, these weapons are difficult to obtain, difficult to use effectively, or both.

To build a bomb capable of producing a nuclear explosion requires so much scientific, manufacturing, and technical infrastructure that only a few nations—and no private organizations—have ever done so. Far easier than deploying an actual nuclear bomb would be for terrorists to steal or buy raw nuclear-weapons material—or even highly radioactive nuclear waste—and package this with a conventional bomb. Imagine the cancers and other radiation-induced illness that might have resulted if one of the airplanes that hit the World Trade Center had been carrying a suitcase full of concentrated uranium or plutonium.

Using chemical weapons for mass destruction presents a different set of problems. They're much easier to buy or make than nuclear weapons, but much harder to deliver in any way that would harm many people. For example, in the 1990s the Japanese cult Aum Shinrikyo tried mightily, with good technical expertise, to poison crowds with nerve gas in the Tokyo subway system but succeeded in killing only twelve people.

Like chemical weapons, biological weapons are easier to acquire than to deliver. Few potentially lethal infectious agents can survive outside a living host long enough to be used as a weapon of mass destruction. Smallpox is the scariest possibility. Humans are the smallpox virus's only host. No humans have been infected with smallpox for decades, and a new epidemic begun today could kill billions around the world. The only known samples of smallpox virus are locked away in labs in the United States and Russia. It is unknown whether other samples are secretly held elsewhere, and if so whether terrorists might be able to acquire them. After September 11, the U.S. government began stockpiling millions of doses of smallpox vaccine, so as to have enough on hand by the end of 2002 to vaccinate every American, if need be.

The infectious agent most likely to be used for terrorism is anthrax, a disease that afflicts livestock around the world, including parts of the western United States. When an animal dies of anthrax, the anthrax bacteria in that animal convert to spores, tiny and very stable carriers of infection. Anthrax spores can lie dormant in soil for decades, waiting for a new host in which to revive and multiply. (Anthrax doesn't spread directly from animal to animal, or human to human.) If anthrax spores work their way into a cut or rash on a person's skin, they can infect that person, resulting in a nasty skin irritation and potentially a life-threatening infection of the whole body. If a person inhales the spores, the infection is far more dangerous. Antibiotic medicines can kill anthrax and save an infected person's life—if treatment is begun early enough.

Anthrax is relatively easy to acquire. Many labs around the world keep samples of it for research into disease prevention and treatment. It is relatively difficult, though, to make anthrax into a weapon. To do that, the bacteria must be produced in large quantities and converted into spores. Then the clumps of spores must be ground very, very fine and treated to reduce static electricity so that instead of sticking together they'll float freely enough to be breathed deep into people's lungs. All of this processing is dangerous and requires technical expertise, time, and money. Beyond all this, the biggest obstacle a would-be anthrax terrorist faces is how to deliver the spores in a way that could infect large numbers of people. No one has ever done that, although several nations' weapons programs have devised ways that might work.

Infecting *small* numbers of people—and frightening millions of others—is much easier, as the events of fall 2001 demonstrated. On October 5, a Florida man who worked for a supermarket tabloid died of inhaled anthrax. His was the first publicly known case of a cluster of anthrax infections apparently related to letters mailed on September 18. Two of those letters were mailed to news organizations in New York, and another was presumably opened and then discarded at the Florida man's office. A second cluster of infections soon followed, these apparently related to two letters (and perhaps others, undetected) mailed on October 9 to U.S. senators' offices in Washington. The anthrax in these letters was concentrated, finely ground, and treated with an antistatic agent, making it highly dangerous. By the end of November, twenty-three people had shown signs of anthrax infection; five had died. Thousands more had certainly or possibly been exposed to anthrax and were taking antibiotics to fight off infection.

Beyond the fact that all four of the recovered anthrax-laced letters were mailed in New Jersey, investigators had no clue as to who sent them. The letters did not, at least at first, appear to be related to the hundreds of anthrax hoaxes mailed to abortion clinics in recent years. Nor was it clear whether the anthrax attacks were in any way related to September 11. Osama bin Laden's organization has in the past reportedly tried to buy nuclear and chemical weapons materials and has experimented with biological and chemical weapons at training camps in Afghanistan. As of early 2002, though, investigators had found no clear link between the fall 2001 anthrax attacks and bin Laden or al-Qaeda.

CHAPTER 7

FIGHTING TERRORISM IN AMERICA

There's no one good way to fight terrorism. Effective counter-terrorism measures can be cheap and easy—or expensive, difficult, inconvenient, and destructive of civil liberties. In a vicious circle, government threats to civil liberties in the name of counterterrorism may actually *encourage* more terrorism, by eroding people's belief in the government's legitimacy and decreasing their willingness to cooperate with law enforcement. To fight the best fight against terrorism, policy makers must weigh costs, benefits, and effectiveness to come up with a set of measures that are acceptable to the American public and do the job well.

Homeland Security

Nine days after the September 11 attacks, amid fears that more attacks might be planned, President George W. Bush announced the creation of a new federal Office of Homeland Security, to be headed by his old friend Tom Ridge, who was then governor of Pennsylvania. The new office would be responsible for both defending against and responding to acts of terrorism in the United States. More than forty federal departments, agencies, and bureaus were involved, from the Central Intelligence Agency and the Defense Department to the FBI and the Centers for Disease Control and Prevention. Governor Ridge would oversee and coordinate their efforts.

The most obvious and immediate problem to be solved was airline security, to guard against future attempts at hijacking similar to what happened on September 11. Prior to September 11 the airlines, not the government, were responsible for maintaining airport security. They contracted the job out, usually to the lowest bidder. As a result, workers at a fast-food restaurant could earn better wages than workers at an airport security checkpoint. After September 11, it seemed obvious that better training, better pay, and better supervision for airport security workers were needed. Other security measures were also suggested: for example, matching luggage to passengers so nobody could check a bag and not board the flight, using more sophisticated scanners for both checked and carry-on luggage, and allowing pilots (many of whom have served in the U.S. military) to carry guns. In late September, while Congress was working on longer-range airport security legislation, President Bush announced several measures that would take effect immediately: National Guard troops would be sent to airports to help out with security, more plainclothes air marshals would fly on commercial flights, and money would be given to the airlines to strengthen cockpit doors and install other security upgrades. In mid-November, Congress passed legislation specifying that federal employees would take over baggage screening and other security at most U.S. airports for at least the next three years.

But might tighter security at airports simply divert terrorists to other targets, other weapons? If passenger jets become tightly guarded, might future terrorists choose instead to steal a cargo jet? Or explode a ship carrying a low-tech bomb (like the one used at Oklahoma City) in a busy harbor? Or target shipments of potentially dangerous industrial chemicals, such as chlorine, shipped in huge quantities every day, all over the country? To completely secure all possible targets and weapons for terrorism would be impossibly expensive and unbearably restrictive. After

A giant
American flag
hangs in
Washington's
Reagan
National
Airport, where
members of
the National
Guard were on
patrol after
September 11.

September 11, law enforcement officials upped security at bridges and train stations, water reservoirs and nuclear power plants. Should we also expect—or accept—tighter security at schools, department stores, even public parks? Under what circumstances is it useful, cost-effective, and acceptable for law enforcement to use video surveillance? To use racial or ethnic profiling to target whole categories of Americans for closer scrutiny? To search hand-bags? To strip-search suspected terrorists?

Like airport security, immigration policy was sharply criticized after September 11. Several of the September 11 suicide hijackers were able to enter and remain in the United States through government error or by abusing immigration rules. (So were several of the 1993 World Trade Center bombing/conspiracy defendants.) Immigration-related security measures had already been authorized by Congress in 1996, but their implementation was delayed because Congress wasn't willing to pay for them and because various government agencies were slow to cooperate. After September 11, the need for these measures was more obvious than ever, particularly for a computer system to check that foreign visitors who legally enter the United States do in fact leave when they are supposed to, another system to monitor foreigners here on student visas, and better access to various "watch lists" and intelligence-gathering efforts for those who issue visas and staff border crossings so they can make sure that suspected terrorists and their supporters don't enter the country. Other, more controversial measures have been proposed, including greater government power to detain foreign visitors and legal immigrants and greater power to deport immigrants based on their political associations.

Terrorism, as distinct from ordinary criminal behavior, has an ideological element. Since the American system of justice doesn't recognize "thought crimes," terrorists have commonly been prosecuted for murder, kidnapping, or making "terroristic threats." Most often they have been nabbed not for actual acts of terror but for robberies to fund their activities, on weapons charges, or for racketeering or criminal conspiracy.

In the weeks after September 11, federal and local law enforcement arrested and detained in jail more than a thousand individuals, mostly foreigners, in connection with the terrorist attacks. As of early February 2002, only one had been publicly charged with crimes related to the September 11 attacks—Zacarias Moussaoui, who allegedly had planned to be the twentieth hijacker. While the identities and charges (if any) against most of those detained were kept secret, the Justice Department acknowledged that many were being held not on criminal charges but for immigration violations or as "material witnesses." According to federal law, the government may hold an American citizen as a material witness only if it convinces a judge that there's good reason to believe that the person knows something that could be important to a criminal investigation *and* that such detention is the only way to ensure that the person will remain available for questioning. The rules for foreigners are looser. Since 1996, the federal government has been allowed to detain noncitizens without getting permission from a judge.

Security involves both law enforcement and information gathering. When the FBI and local police are asked not only to bring criminals to justice but also to investigate people with an eye to preventing crime, freedoms are threatened—freedom of association and assembly, freedom of speech, and the fundamental freedom to be left alone. That's why the U.S. Constitution restricts the government's power to imprison material witnesses and to spy on Americans. Some of the measures proposed after September 11 to improve security through better intelligence carry little threat to freedom: For example, its hard to argue with spending more money to better use information already being gathered overseas, which often sits in files untranslated or unseen by those able to make sense of it or use it.

Other measures are more problematic: The Bush administration has asserted that law enforcement may monitor conversations between terrorism suspects and their lawyers, and that foreigners suspected by the president of involvement with terrorism may be tried not in American courts but in secret military tribunals, under rules that favor the prosecution and with no right of appeal to any court, even if the death penalty is imposed. Even some U.S. allies consider such measures to be violations of basic human rights. Spain, for example, in late November announced that it would not send terrorism suspects it held to the United States for trial without assurance that the accused would be tried in a normal civilian court.

Another controversial security measure discussed after September 11 is national identification cards. It would be possible, and not terribly expensive, to issue each person in the United States a card, similar to a drivers license, encoded with both personal information (at least name and address) and biometric data unique to that person (a fingerprint or an eye, voice, or facial pattern). An electronic reading device installed at any security checkpoint—at airports, courthouses, train stations, even schools and hospitals and department stores—could verify that the person is carrying his or her own card and is authorized to get past the checkpoint. Such cards would obviously be useful and cost-effective for speeding up and enhancing security check—without discriminatory ethnic profiling or intrusive questioning and searches. But putting such a system in place would *cost* us civil rights and personal freedom as well. Being compelled to carry identification and justify our presence while going about our normal business would infringe on the implied Constitutional "right to be left alone" and erode the presumption of innocence that's central to the American system of justice. And consider the computer network such a system would have—a network that would record when and where you pass through security checkpoints, perhaps many times a day. What personal information would be included on each card and perhaps logged at each checkpoint? Who would be allowed to see this information? For what purposes might it be used?

In late October 2001, Congress passed and President Bush signed a law giving the government more powers to investigate and fight terrorism. Highlights of the new law include the following:

- Bringing the government's surveillance powers up to date with new technology, by allowing a special court to authorize listening in when a suspect talks on any phone (rather than authorizing wiretaps on specific phone lines, as in the past) and by allowing court orders for monitoring e-mail similar to those used for phone conversations.
- Increasing the government's power to detain without charge immigrants suspected of involvement with terrorism.
- Allowing law enforcement officials (whose activities are closely scrutinized by courts) and intelligence officials (who are freer to do things courts might frown upon) to share information.
- Granting government greater powers to crack down on money laundering and other loosely regulated banking practices useful in funding terrorism.

What Kind of America?

The fight against terrorism calls into question what kind of country America will be. American ideals such as a fair justice system, freedom of association, and the fundamental right to be left alone can all be threatened by "homeland defense" efforts. Similarly, the secrecy required to fight a war (to protect U.S. soldiers and hide information useful to an enemy) is itself an enemy of democracy—and in the long run an enemy of the war effort itself. Especially in a war that's likely to be long, with the most important victories (prevention of acts of terror) being quiet rather than obviously heroic, the American public needs enough information to discuss and understand what's going on—a necessary condition for maintaining public support for the war effort.

Part of this public discussion will address ways in which America's actions abroad have unintentionally empowered terrorists. America's traditional embrace of the ideal of freedom has been, and still is, powerfully attractive to people living with little freedom all over the world. Nonetheless, the United States has often failed to support freedom and democracy abroad and instead backed corrupt and repressive governments that have been willing to be our allies and to allow U.S. businesses to make money in their countries. The United States has also opposed restrictions on the widespread sale of weapons (a big business for companies based in the United States and other developed countries), making it cheap and easy for terrorists to arm themselves. In the future, the American public might consider these and other such factors when their elected officials negotiate trade and other international agreements and dispense foreign aid.

In the foreign policy sphere, better security may mean less national sovereignty. Conservative Republicans have been leery of signing on to international agreements that would limit the U.S. government's own power. For example, they've opposed establishment of a permanent international criminal court that would be empowered to try Americans as well as suspects from other nations, and they've opposed biological and other weapons control agreements that would ban U.S. sales or production of certain kinds of weapons or would require inspection of U.S. weapons facilities and research centers by foreigners. But these same measures could fight terrorism by uniting many nations in efforts to bring terrorists to justice and by reducing the supply of weapons. The American public may, after September 11, decide that some such measures would buy enough added security to be worthwhile.

Fighting terrorism has to be improvised as we go along, balancing the costs and benefits of various combinations of policies and tactics, and changing them as circumstances change. Security experts can advise us on what the government might do and how we might change the way we live our lives in order to be safer. But in the United States the ultimate authority and responsibility for deciding what's best—not simply what's safest—belongs not to experts or even to the government but to all of us, collectively in how we choose to vote and individually in how we choose to live.

CHRONOLOGY

November 1979: Islamic student militants take fifty-three Americans hostage at U.S. embassy in Iran.

1988: In Afghanistan, Osama bin Laden and associates form the terrorist organization al-Qaeda.

December 1988: Terrorists sponsored by Libya blow up an American airliner over Lockerbie, Scotland.

February 1993: Truck bomb planted by Islamic militants explodes at World Trade Center in New York.

April 1995: Truck bomb planted by antigovernment extremists affiliated with the U.S. militia movement explodes in Oklahoma City, killing 168.

April 1996: America's longest-running terrorist campaign ends with the arrest of the Unabomber, Theodore Kaczynski.

February 1998: Osama bin Laden extends his "holy war" against the United States, declaring that Muslims should kill U.S. civilians as well as soldiers.

August 1998: Truck bombs planted by associates of Osama bin Laden and al-Qaeda explode outside U.S. embassies in Kenya and Tanzania, killing 223.

October 2000: Terrorists linked to al-Qaeda explode a boat full of explosives alongside the *U.S.S. Cole* in Yemen.

September 11, 2001: Terrorists crash airplanes into World Trade Center and Pentagon, killing more than 4,000.

October 5, 2001: Florida man dies of anthrax infection, the first death among those exposed to anthrax in letters sent by terrorists in September and October.

October 7, 2001: United States begins bombing Afghanistan, which harbors Osama bin Laden.

FOR FURTHER READING

Andryszewski, Tricia, *The Militia Movement in America: Before and After Oklahoma City*. Brookfield, CT: Millbrook Press, 1996.

Fridell, Ron, *Terrorism: Political Violence at Home and Abroad*. Hillside, NJ: Enslow Publishers, 2001.

Gaines, Ann Graham, *Terrorism*. Broomal, PA: Chelsea House, 1998.

Gay, Kathlyn, *Silent Death: The Threat of Chemical and Biological Terrorism*. Brookfield, CT: Twenty-First Century Books, 2001.

Greenberg, Keith, *Terrorism: The New Menace*. Brookfield, CT: Millbrook Press, 1994.

Sherrow, Victoria, *The Oklahoma City Bombing: Terror in the Heartland*. Hillside, NJ: Enslow Publishers, 1998.

Sherrow, Victoria, *The World Trade Center Bombing*. Hillside, NJ: Enslow Publishers, 1998.

INDEX

El-Gabrowny, Ibrahim, 22
Environmental movement, 10, 27

FALN, 12
Farah Diba, Empress, *14*
Federal Bureau of Investigation
    (FBI), 25, 51, 55
Federal gun-control legislation, 30,
    31
Foreign aid, 58
French Revolution, 16

Gun control, 28, 30, 31

Hitler, Adolf, 26
Holland Tunnel, New York City, 21
Homeland security, 51–52, *53*, 54–57
Hussein, Saddam, 18

Immigration policy, 54
Industrial chemicals, 52
International criminal court, 58
Iran, 13–15, 16, 35–36, 47
    hostage crisis (1979), 13, 15
Iraq, 16, 18, 46
Islam, 14, 15, 18, 21, 35–36, 45
Israel, 15, 18, 21, 35

Japan, 48
Jews, 10, 28
Jihad ("holy war"), 15
Jordan, 35, 36, 38, 42
Justice, U.S. Department of, 55

Kabul, Afghanistan, 47
Kaczynski, Theodore J., 27, *27*
Kahane, Rabbi Meir, 21, 22
Kandahar, Afghanistan, 47
Kenya, 34
Khomeini, Ayatollah Ruhollah, 14,
    15

Ku Klux Klan (KKK), 8–10, *9*, 25, 28

La Belle nightclub, Berlin,
    Germany, 16, *17*
LaGuardia Airport, New York, 12
Latin America, 12
Leaderless resistance organization,
    30–31, 38, 41
Leftist revolutionaries, 10–11
Libya, 16, 18
Lincoln Tunnel, New York City, 21
Lockerbie, Scotland, 16, 18
Lynchings, 10

Mathews, Robert, 26
McVeigh, Timothy James, 31–32
Military tribunals, 56
Militia movement, 27–28, *29*, 30–32
Millennium bombing plot, Jordan,
    35, 36, 38, 42
Mohammad Reza Shah Pahlavi,
    13–14, *14*
Money laundering, 57
Moussaoui, Zacarias, 55
Mubarak, Hosni, 21
Muhammad, Prophet, 36
Musharraf, Pervez, 45, *46*

Nairobi, Kenya, 34
National Guard, 52, *53*
National identification cards, 56
Neo-Nazis, 25, 26
New York area landmarks, 21, 42
New York Federal Building, 21
New York Stock Exchange, 43
Nichols, Terry Lynn, 32
North Atlantic Treaty Organization
    (NATO), 45
North Korea, 47
Nosair, El Sayyid A., 21, 22
Nuclear weapons, 48, 50